Through the eyes of a schizophrenic.
Film script written by Gavin Scott Hughes.

Narrator, (God's voice.)

After I designed the planet, I decided I would create Adam and Eve. I also decided that there would be many chosen ones, so many per generation that would do my work and give empty vessels, people without my word the information guidance and protection that so many now need.

Special Effects.

The rain is falling but it isn't rain, it's eyes, ears, noses and mouths. Plus thousands of electrical items e.g tv's, radios etc. The trees all have their own personalities and they are holding highly intelligent conversation complete with emotions. They are also questioning what God is saying along with the domesticated animals and other wildlife.

It's also thundering and lightning and God appears to be playing the drums, the drums representing the thunder and his disco lights representing the lightning. Then he starts to party has a few drinks and pours the Holy spirit onto Earth and this is the rain.

Narrator, (God's voice.)

And so I placed Schizophrenics Manic Depressives, Schizo effective disorders, psychic powers etc to help defeat the wicked one, his fallen angels also his followers. As the story of mankind begins I warn you do not watch this film if you are bothere at all about the powers of good and evil.

Special Effects.

1st soundtrack, Oasis (champagne supernova). Screen goes black.
2nd soundtrack, Toni Braxton (How could an angel break my heart). Screen goes white.

Both to be played at a reasonable volume.

Narrator, (God's voice.)

Together we learn to reunite for life is after all black and white.

Scene 1.

Theres an opening in the forest where a mother, a virgin, called Herma and a carpenter Stephen who are having a son they did not necessarily mean to have named Gavin and he would take his full name of Gavin Scott Hughes.
 Gavins' black family on his mothers side, his grandfather Luther, his grandmother Beatrice, his 8 aunties, one of them being Gavins fairy godmother. His uncle Phillip is also present. Gavins' white side of the family, Morgan and Jean his grandparents and his 2 uncles Mark and homosexual Paul are all present at the arrival of the new born King. The year is 1977 the year of the Golden Jubilee.

Scene 2.

The family are all squabbling over Gavin the new born baby.

<u>Stephen:</u> I hold this baby up in the air, he's my son and I'm going to call him Cunte cunte you cunts.

Scene 3.

Stephen holds Gavin and squeezes his head almost as if to shape it like a peanut.

<u>Stephen:</u> He's my fucking son, fuck off the lot a ya do one!

Scene 4.

<u>Herma:</u> Just pass me my fucking baby now Stephen! Leave your hooligan yobbo mentality at 43 Loverton Road, Acocks Green where it belongs!

Jean: Let me have a hold of my grandson. Is he going to stay white like this? Will his hair stay straight? Will he get darker Marcia? (Jean often refers to Herma as Marcia because that was the name Dad had told mom to tell his parents.)

Herma: I don't want that baby, he hasn't come out of me, I've had an alien! (Herma refuses to believe Gavin is her son because he had been born so light skinned.)

Scene 5.

Narrator, (God's voice.)

At this point both families are willing to explode and start arguing, a fight breaks out over Gavin the mixed race baby due to a very heated argument as to who would take on the new baby boy.

Stephen: Okay for fucks sake lets just get him home and get him fed for his needs are more important.

Scene 6.

Narrator, (God's voice.)

Gavin arrives home at 85 Francis road, Erdington, Birmingham screaming and crying the best he could because his father had squeezed his new born baby sons's head so hard he had felt the two fingerprints either side.

Luther: Boy, come ya now! Mek yuh grandfather get rid of yuh bad cough that you have! (Luther gives Gavin a suck on his pipe and a drop of white rum. Gavin brings up some flem.)

Beatrice: Lord God! See what Luther has done, he has got the baby's chest better.

Narrator, (God's voice.)

Everyone in the Whytes' and Hughes' family all take it in turns to hold baby Gavin. They start telling him stories and try comforting him to take his first look at the world where he was about to grow up in.

Scene 7.

Narrator, (God's voice.)

It has been some time now around 4 years and Gavin is very boisterous at this toddler stage of his development. He is going through having chicken pox and goes to stay with his nanny Whyte, Beatrice. Gavin takes a great interest in a documentary called, once upon a time man. Gavin and his nan would watch films together and this was what was to come, a very kind and loving relationship. Not to mention with a few bad pointers.

Gavin: When is it coming on again nan?

Beatrice: You want to see it again and it's only just finished, come on now son take your medicine.

Gavin gives a Beatrice a look as if to say I don't need medicine nan I'm ok.

Scene 8.

Narrator, (God's voice.)

Herma and Steve come back from a hard days work. Herma being a secretary and Steve being a window cleaner.

Herma: How's my son mom?

Beatrice: Well he is fine when did you say you were coming back? 5 hours ago? At least you have finally arrived Lord God the boy is really unwell. He has only had a little curry goat and rice from morning,

Herma: Well it's better than what we got. Say goodbye to grandmother Gavin.

Gavin: Bye bye nanna.

Steve: Old biddy she's the dirtiest breed on the fucking planet Herma. I know it's ya mom but I just don't like her at all for fuck sake.

Scene 9.

Narrator, (God's voice.)

Beatrice keeps sending her seven daughters and brother round to keep a close eye on the newly wed couple. Although the wedding itself was nothing to write home about. Herma and Steve had snuck off to get married in a registry office on Broad street, Birmingham. The wedding was never blessed due to both of their parents not wanting or tolerating a mixed marriage.

Scene 10.

Steve: You give em an inch and they take a mile Herma why won't they just let us get on with it? Just because we are a young black and white couple? We are married what's their fucking problem? Have we been cursed or something?

Herma: Don't worry Steve all we have to do is stay strong we will make it! It's just the black and white issue that's all.

Steve: Well fuck that Herma you stop at home with the kids and let me go out and be the bread winner.

A little thought bubble appears over Herma's head. It reads hang on who have I really married here? He wants me to stay here and be a housewife. How many qualifications have I got? How many has he got? He's having a laugh.

Steve: You taking the piss Herma! Washing up needs to be done, we are in a council flat! The sweeping too, we have also got Gavin to consider now which is an extra responsibility. Don't be funny with me cause I'm no cunt!

Scene 11.

Narrator, (God's voice.)

By this time Herma and Steve are feeling the frustrations of being a mixed couple and a few people in the neighbourhood were not only hassling them but also wishing bad things on them. On their relationship like I hope when your kids are older they all die. Yet Herma and Steve were determined to make things work between them.

Sandra: (Herma's sister) Come Herma you need to come up to the house. Mom's saying that you slept with dad.

Herma: WHAT!? Ok give me five minutes.

Steve: If it ain't one thing it's the fucking other what the fuck is going on? All I want is a peacefull life, me, my wife and kids.

Scene 12.

Narrator, (God's voice.)

Herma goes up to her mom's house to find Beatrice and Luther having a very heated conversation. The truth comes out about Luther interfering with his daughter Herma and the family breaks up. Grandfather Luther decides to live with his other daughter Marva for a bit till all dies down. The seven sisters and one brother are glad to see Luther home and welcome him to the fact he is in good health. However not long after this Luther contracts an awful cough that causes one of his lungs to burst and he is rushed into hospital for emergency surgery.

Scene 13.

Dr Inman: This has totally baffled and confused medical scientists Mr Whyte by rights you shouldn't be breathing now let alone walk all the way home as you did. I will consult a consultant for more information.

Luther looking somewhat troubled by what the doctor has said laughs with relief as he often used to do before his tragic death in the early 90's. God rest his soul.

Luther: Thankyou doctor how long do I have left?

Dr Inman: A big strong man like you need not worry about that yet not until nearer the time, your as strong as an ox as they often say medically your health never seizes to amaze me. I'll make another appointment.

Scene 14.

Narrator, (God's voice.)

Herma collects her father from the surgery.

Herma: How are you dad? Feeling any better?

Luther: Yes thank you, don't ask your father questions, deaf ears mary.

Herma: I was only concerned that's all. What did the doctor say are you? I mean will you be okay or did he say it was serious?

Luther: Dem say what don't kill you we fatten you no true sah?

Scene 15.

Narrator, (God's voice.)

Herma is now back at home where Steve and Gavin are waiting for her to prepare a meal for all. Gavin is now saying his first words and taking his first steps.

Gavin: Dadda work, dadda bus, dadda look mommy mommy, daddy birdy.

Steve: I'm going to start taking that little cunt to work with me.

Herma: You wish!

Steve: Oh you will see he can come on the motor bike.

Herma: He's only a baby Ste.

Steve: He's no ordinary baby he's a Hughes and don't you ever forget it as long as you live. How you doing matey you daddy's little boy ay! Arr have some of that get it down your neck. (Steve gives Gavin some alcohol.)

Scene 16.

Narrator, (God's voice.)

Gavin had been watching Evil Knievil on television so he decided to copy a stunt down the stairs on his brand new bicycle. Unfortunatly Gavin was too young to understand the seriousness involved in doing a stunt like that down a maisonette block staircase. So as expected Gavin suffers a nasty fall. Herma and Steve hear the cries and then remembered that they had left a toddler unattended in the block. Gavin runs in and now takes a bottle of baby powder and pours it all over his baby brother Wesley who is 1 year and three months younger than Gavin. People often mistake them for twins as the story goes on.

Scene 17.

Steve: You know what I think we should do Herma? Buy a car they are a lot more sensible than bikes and safer. Plus we have the two boys now and who knows how many will follow. I feel it's the best move to make honestly Herm.

Herma: Well I guess it is but lets take one step at a time I don't want you boxing no more now we have a family and I guess as long as it gets us from A to B it shouldn't be a problem.

Narrator, (God's voice.)

So Herma gets herself a Daihatsu and Steve got himself a cortina subsequently selling the motorbike. He also thinks about quitting professional lightweight boxing.

Scene 18.

<u>Steve:</u> I tell you what Herma, I just need to hit some cunt. I've just fought a profesional fight in Liverpool got stopped on cuts and that fucking Ernie Cashmore picked me up in a top of the range Rolls Royce. I tell you what look at the rarse purse £500.00 to pussybag who the fuck is he taking me for a fucking muppet!

<u>Herma:</u> I told you Steve you not only have me to consider you have Gavin, Wesley and Debbie on the way. We have a three bedroomed house to keep up, we are no longer in a flat. Come on this is Chudleigh road lets make the most of it. You take on a building and construction apprenticeship and I will take care of the house and kids. We have got nothing to lose let's give it our best shot.

Scene 19.

<u>Beatrice:</u> Them working class shit house them, they are not in our class they are not used to food, we are used to land's and houses farming tell dem Luther you was fed as a child.

<u>Luther:</u> B them deh children dem a try a little way in a life love dem mek dem gwarn, I know Steve is white but him a good man and him a deserve a chance. Me like da boy for der is something special bout him. You see what really happen is I really feel he is psychic like me B.

<u>Beatrice:</u> Oh Luther stop talking those foolishness there, how is the young boy supposed to look after Herma? He is dyslexic Herma has her qualifications her life ahead of her. About say the boy is psychic Luther now you listen to me both yourself and I, Jean and Morgan do not agree for a mixed marriage. If you do not recieve your parent's blessing than the Bible says the marriage cannot go ahead

or be sanctioned in the sight of the almighty God whom art in heaven.

Luther: B I am trying to talk will you not hear what I'm trying to tell you. Shut your big mouth and let me finish what I'm saying,

Beatrice: All right then but I won't give up untill that good for nothing working class shit house is out of my families lives for good and I mean good!

Scene 20.

Narrator, (God's voice.)

Back to Herma's household where they have just had Herma's siblings arrive.

Herma: Come in, make yourselves at home.

Steve: Oh for fucks sake I can't believe my fucking eyes, give em an inch and they take a mile! All they are doing is going backwards and forwards to your parents Herma. Can't you see that you thick cunt?

Herma cuts her eye at Steve and sucks her teeth.

Herma: How are you all doing? Steve has got some cheap meat and I have groceries in the cupboard just help yourselves don't mind the nasty white boy go ahead.

Steve: It's for you me and the kids Herma for fuck sake! What are they trying to do eat me out of house and home? I go to work all my life to be taken for a cunt by your family! Who were all spoon fed all there fucking lives! Herma do you know what it's like growing up with a family in Dublin? We were raised on dry bread and water, our pudding was fucking toast and dripping! Your not in Jamaica now! It's England, do you think the streets are paved with gold? Hear me when I speak I've got no respect in my own fucking home. Hear me!

Herma: Listen to him major identity crisis or what! He thinks he is black!

Herma and her siblings start making fun of Steve, laughin at him.

Steve: That's it! I'm fucking off out!

Gavin and Wesley: Where's daddy going? Mummy we want to go too why can't we go?

Herma: Oh shut up and go to your fucking beds!

Herma beats and whips Gavin and Wesley, they run off crying to bed hoping to see their father soon.

Scene 21.

Narrator, (God's voice.)

Steve returns with Luther.

Herma: So where have you been? Over to one of your womans houses?

Steve: Look just wake the kids up for me we have been to my parents to get the kids' christmas presents after all it is christmas even if you don't celebrate it.

Herma: Come down here now kids! Your father is speaking to you! NOW!

Luther: Boy Stevey boy I don;t know what you and Herma have but you need to sort out your problems.

Steve: Tell me about it Luth I love ya haha.

Special Effects.

Soundtrack, Kenny Rogers (Lucille), to be played softly.

Luther: Now unuh pitney go round a unuh mother now an when I catch unuh backside tonight you see man a gwarn warm it, bust it an give unuh a real good rarsing tonight ya!

Scene 22.

Narrator, (God's voice.)

Herma's siblings scarper for their livs back to 85 Francis road and run all the way as they fear their father Luther greatly.

Beatrice: I did tell you children not to interfere in a man and womans argument! Now, tell me what is happening round Herma and Steve's? How is Gavin and Wesley keepng? You see Herma is now pregnant again with a girl child. Steve would not even give her time to heal up from the first two never mind him goin to breed her up again! Lord God!

Special Effects.

Soundtrack to be played reasonably high, What a friend we have in jesus (gospel version).

Scene 23.

Narrator, (God's voice.)

Back at Chudleigh Road Gavin and Wesley are opening their presents they had been bought by their father and grandfather Luther.

Gavin: Wow look Wesley I got the Incredible Hulk!

Wesley: Gavin look what I got it's a tonka toy!

Gavin: So, look what I got Action Man and B.A Barocus.

Wesley: We have loads of toys Gavin I hope our cousins don't take them all off us you know what they are like!

Steve: Go on give your brother a love, Gav go on, Wes give Gav a love!

Herma: Just shut up moron I don't know why I ever had kids with you in the first place! Never in my life did I think I'd meet a white man that would be convinced he was black! You dutty bumboclart rarseclart a come tell me father me business, how di rarse you fi do that how you fi mention dat a soh me know say some man a play number two an a fuck mans bottom! Gavin an Wesley mek yuh father tell yuh bout him homosexual brother yuh AUNTY Paul!

Steve: Yeh! What ever you black wog that's why I joined BNP so I could go round bashing pakies and fucking up black wogs like you!

Herma: Whatever! Whatever! Steve I'm gonna teach you a fucking valuable lesson, listen to me I did not marry you because I loved you! You were a lyer and a theif, a murder, arsonist and you held me, beat me up and raped me on Hobmoor Rd, Yardley Wood, Birmingham.

Steve: Herma, we had our 2 boys out of love and our daughter on the way will be born out of love!

Herma: You stay there believing that Steve! Gavin and Wesley and Deborrah Terresah were all concieved by way of rape. You raped me Steve! Constantly! I will remind you of this for the rest of your life you white honkey.

Steve: For fuck sake after the way I've treated you! You mad bastard, kids fuck off to bed!

Scene 24.

Narrator, (God's voice.)

Steve kicks and punches Herma in a state of murderous intent and Herma cries out blue murder meanwhile Gavin and Wesley are upstairs hearing their pregnant mother being beaten to a pulp by their evil father.

Scene 25.

Narrator, (God's voice.)

Herma is crying as Steve has beaten her senseless and is not aware of his own strength. Steve shouts out right where's my dinner and as Herma is preparing the corned beef and rice she cuts herself on the corned beef. Steve panics and calls an ambulance. As Herma leaves Gavin and Wesley are at the top of the stairs.

Gavin and Wesley: Where's mommy going Dad? Tell us! Tell us!

Stephen: Fuck off you black wogs, your doing my fucking head in. Do one bed now! Fuck off to bed now! you load of black fucking cunts. Fuck off now!

Scene 26.

Narrator, (God's voice.)

Steve starts punching and headbutting and smashing the entire house to pieces.

Scene 27.

Narrator, (God's voice.)

Later that night Herma returns from hospital after being heavily sedated and tranquilised and falls to sleep in Steve and hers marital bed. This is around 10 on the night. At 2am Steve wakes Herma.

Steve: Wake up Herma quickly there's something moving acroos the room!

Herma: Oh ssshhh Steve go back to sleep!

Steve: No honestly Herma please quick look! LOOK!

Scene 28.

Herma looks across the room and is amazed as what Steve could see had now walked on the creaky floorboard near to the bedroom door. An evil spirit was in the house, the house being demon possessed and as expected Steve and Herma both gazed at each other totally amazed.

Scene 29.

Narrator, (God's voice.)

Meanwhile in Gavin and Wesley's room, Gavin wakes and wakes up his brother to say,

Gavin: Wes I can hear something coming down the landing, I wonder if it's dad or mom?

Wesley: I dunno Gav probably let's get some sleep bro we have been talking all night.

Scene 30.

Narrator, (God's voice.)

Suddenly there's a great crashing sound of broken glass as the evil spirit smashes through the bedroom window where Gavin and Wesley slept at night.

Gavin: Come on Wes let's go and sleep in mom and dad's room even if we sleep at the bottom of the bed at least the demons and devil will not get us, not that easily anyway!

Wesley: Listen! There's a cat screaming frantically out in the back garden! Bloody hell!

Soundtrack 1, 2 Freddy's coming for you played medium volume.

Steve: What's that boys? Hey lads!

Gavin and Wesley: The devil is in our home dad.

Scene 31.

Narrator, (God's voice.)

Steve laughs, Herma is in a great deal of shock yet very lethargic due to the medication the doctors had gave her.

Herma: Just go back to sleep sons, I'll see you both in the morning, come on Steve stop messing around, don't frighten them.

Scene 32.

Narrator, (God's voice.)

Herma decides to sell the house as both herself and Steve at this point have realised that the house must have been built on some type of ancient witch burial ground or something along those lines. Either way they wern't staying there.

Scene 33.

Narrator, (God's voice.)

Herma and Steve go to the estate agents enquiring about a new property as they wern't hanging about to find out the reasons for the strange happening at the old house. Luckily enough they both found a property they could both afford at Neville Rd, Erdington. Even though the mortgage price was high they decided to move anyway.

Steve: It's alright ain't it Herms?

Herma: Sure is! Check the attic, who knows they night have left some valuables behind after all they have left all their furniture.

Gavin, Wesley and Debbie: It's alright aint it! Look at this mom and dad!

Scene 34.

Narrator, (God's voice.)

Herma, Steve and the boys also the recent arrival, in her fifth year of life Deborah gets on with moving their belongings from the old house to the new one. Beatrice arrives with Herma's 8 siblings in tow.

Beatrice: But then tell me Herma you are doing well for yourself now aren't you? Without you Steve would be nothing, an absolute zero on the map, is this not so?

Herma: You know mom the man is just too slow to understand things. No matter how I tell him to read and write it's as if he just has no respect for education what so ever!

Claudine: I don't know what you see in that hooligan yobbo. He has a yard mentality that man has. Herma find yourself a black man just get rid of that idiot.

Marva: I'm saying nothing I'll just listen.

Nadia: Well it is plain to see swiftly moving on the guys an absolute moron. Move on Herma just get rid of him!

Sandra: Well there's no way I'd even lower myself to sleep with a white man no matter whether he was thick like Steve or intelligent. There's just no fucking way, nothings changed mother seems like you ain't the full shilling Herma!

Lorna: Come on give him a chance he has done nothing wrong that's just men for ya!

Wilma: I just can't bear the thought of having a white man, even the thought of it! They can't cook, they smell and they have small dicks. They're nasty they don't even know who their parents are! Most of them were raised in children's homes and they are bastards in the true sense of the word. Illegitamates born out of wedlock!

Gwendoline: I agree with some of what you are all saying but he has a big penis for a white man and he's the only white man that is convinced he's black and speaks patwa so well I mean how can I complain?

Phillip: I don't know what to say I mean Herma at the end of the day if you would have listened to mom and dad all this trouble that you are in now could have all been avoided. Not only that Steve's parents told you both the same thing did they not and no doubt I know you are the oldest but I think things will only get worse staying in that sort of marriage. What do you honestly think Herma? Come on be truthful?

Herma: True still, you know Phillip when you speak to me like that you remind me of dad and how he would handle it. Do you know what I'm saying? I can only agree sometimes I am a bit too deaf for my own good.

Special Effects.

Soundtracks to be played softly mixed into the background.

1, Toni Braxton, How could an angel break my heart.

2, Ub40 Homely girl.
3, Ken Boothe, Everything I own.
4, Jamelia, Thank you.
5, Sinead O Connor, Nothing compares to you.

Scene 35.

Narrator, (God's voice.)

So Herma took her families advice and decided she would take a 6 month break away from her husband and children. She had not long had Sadie So now there was four children. Sadie being the last one on the list due to an ectopic pregnancy that Herma would suffer after she had had Sadie. When Herma returned to England after her well deserved 6 month break she had met someone new called Henry alias Marger and how happy she was. Gavin was 12 around this time.

Gavin: Mom, what was it like in Jamaica? How was it?

Herma: Fuck off and go away you little half breed rarse!

Gavin: But mom at least tell me what the beaches and the caribbean waters looked like come on mom! Cheer up! What's wrong?

Herma: It was nice now go back to your dad's house, your dad lives at 122 Neville Road this is my house in Kings Road! Fuck off I have no children.

Gavin: Mom I'm gonna go and tell dad somethings wrong, I know it is, you don't seem like my normal mom to me.

Herma: Go to your dad's now!

Narrator, (God's voice.)

It seemed almost as if when Herma had gone to Jamaica someone had spiked her drink in a bar so that they could talk her into bringing all her riches to Jamaica from England.

Funnily enough 6 months later that is exactly what Herma did only this time taking her 4 children with her. She sold three properties and took that cash too. She was now deeply in love with Henry Sland alias Marger. during the six month period prior to going to Jamaica, Herma and Steve had the children constantly backwarding and forwarding as if they were using their own children to carry messages like pigeons. the fights and arguing were out of this world.

Special effects.

Soundtrack John Lennon, Imagine. To be played softly.

Gavin is in Steve's car having a chat.

<u>Steve:</u> How you doing son? Are you ok? What has your mom been up to?

<u>Gavin:</u> I don't know dad but I think we are all going to live in Jamaica.

Steve: You fucking what?

Gavin: Don't get angry dad it's just the way things go sometimes that's all. We will all come back soon, how do you think I feel dad? I'm going to leave behind my friends, girlfriends, school life everything I've ever had is going to be left behind. Mom has also got deeply into the Jehovah's witness thing and it's doing everyones head in!

Steve: I'm not on about you am I? I'm talking about your mom, has she got someone new? A black man? Tell me now you black cunt, now fucking trap off!

Scene 36.

Narrator, (God's voice.)

Meanwhile in 42 kings road Herma and her siblings and children are awaiting the arrival of Gavin. They wish to hear about the conversation Gavin had just had with his father. Gavin and Steve make their way into the house, Steve looks anxious to hear about the move to Jamaica, he also is trying hard to get his marriage and life back together.

Special effects.

Soundtracks to be played softly and in background.

1, Dr Hook (Sylvia's mother).
2, Simon & Garfunkel, (The boxer).
3, I remember Dublin city in the rare old times, (rebel version).
4, Paddy look back, (rebel version).
5, Kingston town, (Ub40).
6, Elvis Presley, (Heart break hotel).
7, Elvis Presley, (Are you lonesome tonight).

A conversation is going to take place where by each person in the room has another person in the room to switch places with not only vocals, while one one person is speaking for another person nobody moves place from their original position. For example Claudine speaks like Herma and vice versa not only do they swap voices they also swap faces and bodies, as the switch happens you can see the different elements of their character going across the room.

Special effects.

Narrator, (God's voice.)

Now there's a big family get together at 42 Kings Road, everyone young and old are enjoying themselves, dancing, romancing, drinking and smoking, the average Jamaican house party. Jokes are being told and Steve is very insecure as he knows that this will probably be no doubt one of the last times we would be together as a family unit.

Special effects.

Soundtracks to be played;

1, Ub40, (Cover up).
2, Kylie Minogue & Jason Donovan, (Especially for you).

3, Percy Sledge, (When a man loves a woman).
4, Reggae version, (On the wings of love).

Scene 37.

Herma: (With Claudine's vocals.) I don't know what Steve was thinking when he decided he was going to leave his drugs and devil worship, BNP to marry a black woman and have mixed race children. For all I can see maybe it was out of revenge, he did want to name Gavin Hitler believe it or not and when I heard the man lose his temper I knew there was never any love there fucking hooligan!

Claudine: (With Phillips vocals and hairstyle.) Well Herms all I can say is you were both told it would never work, it was too soon for back and white to mix.

Phillip: (With Sandra's vocals, face and body.) Well erm Herms I don't know exactly what's going on like but personally look what

Steve's done to me like I was working with him trying to earn a bit of bunce and he gets me sectioned under the Mental Health Act! Now I'm a right yampy cunt dya know what I mean like, it's just his silly sense of humour ain't it? Fuck me I can't get no pussy, can't get a job and a fucking life is out of the question! I'm a big black coward whose now classed as Frank Bruno dead from the neck up for fucks sake!

Sandra: (With Mike Tyson's vocals.) Well you see I'm the best talker in the whole wide world, I know everything although I look like Mike Tyson I'm not! Although I am the best prostitute in the world that's not going to stop me from making my millions. When they come they come, I don't wish to elaborate you know it's like right through history. The black woman and black man has been taken for fools. Voodoo, witch doctors and scientists. Anyway I'm just doing sales you know, I don't know why they're terrified of me.

Gwendoline: (With a sumo wrestlers appearance.) Well you see what really happen is the Lord God is good and I feel to myself being the fat bastard I am, it is time for the family to stop inter breeding to keep money and lands in the family. I really feel to myself you see that the real problem here is lack of communication and after all blood is thicker than water. God's mercy is everlasting. his goodness goes out to many generations and Jesus loves you as much as he loves any other fat bastard.

Wilma: (With an italian accent and Steve's eyes and hair). Well Herma it's for the family there need not be no more drugs no more coke, no more blood shed, we have to get down to see the Catholic Father. £60,000 of net profit this year the family are doing well. The cannabis and olive plantation is doing very well. The cocaine farm in Columbia is doing well puro puro puro. As I'm snorting cocaine I feel to myself what's life about? Steve's going to sleep with the fishes.

Nadia: (Thinks she is an African zulu warrior). I think these things are parables of longtime African rebels betrayed by their own, no longer we sit on our thrones, we spend the queens pound, we respect the palace and crowns. We need an M.B.E so we can party, drink overproof rum and Scottish whisky. If we catch a cold we can drink brandy and all this crap between you and Steve is so far fetched I do not believe! Sort yourselves out do you want to set up your own business? Mind your own fucking business!

Special effects.

Soundtracks to be played softly.
1, Sometimes it's hard to be a woman.
2, Noone in the world to hold me.
3, All woman.
4, The words get in the way, (Gloria Estefan).
5, He wasn't man enough for me, (Toni Braxton).

Steve: (Who thinks he's black). Yes you bloodclarts me did tell unuh you cunt! Your a total muppet an I've been one myself so who better to know? Get a tot down ya neck do you want the fucking row? What are you thick? I said I don't want to remember Dublin city ya fucking heaps a shits. Fuck off and leave me the fuck alone! It's me father roots for fucking Ireland!

Lorna: Come on now Steve, calm down do you trust in my father the Lord God my heavenly father that is?

Steve: Of course I do.

Lorna: Well Steve God is good and if you are saved baptised and born again you will get the chance through prayer to gain the opportunity to see your wife, four children again and remember you now have a fifth, a son called Austin for a woman you know, Illegitamate.

Marva: Well Steve, Herma, Claudine, Sandra, Wilma, Gwen and Phillip I am asking if someone will actually listen to me?

Everyone: SHUT UP! Marva you thick girl stop trying to act intelligent that's your main problem in life just act thick like the thick bitch you are!

Marva: Alright then I didn't hear, see say or do anything. I know nothing.

Special effects.

Soundtracks to be played loudly.
1, Michael Jackson, You are not alone.
2, Michael Jackson, Thriller.
3, Queen, Bohemian Rhapsody.

Ricky: (Sandra's boyfriend.) Well, San do you want to come in the garden with me? I've brought some mates along! Are you on or off?

Sandra: I'm off!

Ricky: Come on then what you waiting for? Sandra's up for grabs come on lads! Get the condoms out! Sandra's about!

<u>Wesley:</u> What's going on Gav? What's up? Are we really going?

<u>Gavin:</u> No, I dunno actually Wes you never know your luck in a big city. I'm going to look for some pussy, I've heard Jillian Rooms got a big one coming!

<u>Wesley:</u> Na Gav gunna go look for some of my mates, I'll meet up with you later, I'm looking forward to the beaches and playing football. Are you Gav? Love you catch up with you soon yeh? Laters.

Scene 38.

<u>Jackie Blake:</u> Hows it going Sandra? Can I get some of Ricky? Haha! Got any weed, coke anything? Te more my teeth stick out the more I feel like Bugs Bunny do you know what I mean Sandra? They've told me I'm a walking disease along with you San. When I look into it though I feel the cannabis is killing the pain. Hows it hanging Ricky?

Ricky: Suck this you fucking whore! Gobble Gobble!

Gavin: Well the seriousness of allegations caused by methods and frustrations of the world and southern hemisphere causing pollution in the atmosphere was both chemical and nuclear. Spreading right across the atmosphere, really take away my fear who shall I fear when Lucifer himself is here? As I clear my throat I leave England and shed a tear. Family and friends rest in peace and remember if I die tonight it's because I fought poor peoples rights. I too came for the sick fought all my life, I'm no muppet.

Tundae: Wesley and Gavin if I drink these rotten eggs and this rum and brandy will I get big and strong? Like superman?

Wesley and Gavin: Course you will just drink it, stop being stupid!

Tundae: Ok, Gav yes I can feel it now have you got a phonebox I can change into superman then can't I? Erm, erm, erm, we, we, we, wes, and ge, ge, ge, Gavin won't I? Hang on, I've got my superman cape I'll be back down in a jiffy! Haha!

Scene 39.

Lee: (Runs an off license.) Well I tell you once I tell you twice I will always befriend you see? What really happen from what I can understand is that the relationship never did a work from the first instant. See it did bad from morning it started raining in the afternoons and in the evening got worse. So what really happen is your mother and father said it would work and when I studied it in university Lord Jesus Christ, friends of sinners, the relationship, marriage and every thing was over. I said don't make me repeat myself you Steve did not respect a good woman.

Anna: (Lee's partner.) Well Lee how me see it is that white and black can mix children and have the best of both worlds. Those mix race

children are not evil theyare good I tell you.
There are enough black and white couples
with mixed children to help them gain
confidence. Their blood is blessed by God
himself Lee.

Delroy: (Anna & Lee's son). True still Mom,
that fucking Dionne always doing my head in
mom about Gavs the hardest in Erdington. I'll
show him, yes I'll set for him he sees me for
an idiot. Cause I can't read or write because
of idiots like that beating me senseless. They
threw a stone at me mom! Then licked out
any sense I had in me. That Gavin with his
big fucking words! I hate him!

Dionne: (Delroy's sister). Just shut up Delroy
what you hating on Gavin for your just
making things worse, we are blood man do
you know what I'm saying? Your just jelous
he's more intelligent than you. Leave him
alone your problem is your making friends
with idiots, stop making a fool out of
yourself. Stop making enemies for yourself,
when you realise keeping a friend like Gavin
will be beneficial for you. The sooner you

will realise how important loyalty to a friend is Delroy! For once in your life try to do something constructive and progresive you just chat complete and utter shit.

Spud: (Delroy's homeless friend). Wha gwan bredrin? How's it going? Half of Erdington fucked your sister what you looking so het up about? I'm gonna do time for Gavin, I swear he is pissing me off about he can have anyone in Erdington! Does he think he's god's gift? I'll soon fuck him up, I'll chop him up, he's no friend of mine, He's young!

Scene 40.

Herma recieves a letter from Kie a notorious yardie with wicked intentions towards Herma and her family and in this letter from Jamaica we learn the following about his intentions.

Narrator, (God's voice.)

Dear Herma, You see wha gwarn now lef ya bumbaclart white pitney dem a pussyclart

England otherwise we ago kill them when time a reach them a reach Jamaica pussyhole! Listen me and listen good, if yuh know tek note a weh meh seh, I gwarn mek sure seh unuh get weh di duck get yuh gwarn get fuck! Lef di bumba suck pussy white boy an carry da maoney come weh me seh Herma? Carry de money come like you no real pussyclart badman original Jamiacan Mafia seh? Kie.

To Herma from Oney, When you pussyhole come back a Jamaica mek sure ya fat rarse no come back round ere. You know seh England people are mad. Come back to Jamaica mek sure ya got ya money and all your possessions dem. You are too materialistic your life is worth more than gold and you are guilty of vanity. Diss me and see what ya bumbaclart will get! I will shoot up a hole inna ya, you know everyone answers to me! Me a bad boy you hear? Oney.

To Herma from Rose, I liked the photos you sent me, Gavin's really good looking and I'm just dying to meet him. Have you told him how attractive I am 5 foot 7 inches tall and I enjoy my school work. He has a cheeky smile and from what I've seen on the photos I'd love to meet him and for him to be my boyfriend, love Rose. See you soon.

Scene 41.

Special effects.

Gavin's daughter Latoya and Latoya's mom Clara appear in the form of angels in Gavin's dream.

Clara: Gavin one day I'll be the mother of your child and this child will be your daughter.

Latoya: Yes daddy this will be me, you will probably see me when I'm a lot older than you expect because mom has plans to have me adopted.

Gavin murmurs in his sleep.

Gavin: Why? Why? Why? Clara don't I want my daughter I want you both here with me!

Clara: Don't worry Gavin go back to sleep now there's a good boy!

Scene 42.

Gavin: Mom, I had the strangest dream about Jamaica last night, it was weird there was a girl called Clara and believe it or not my daughter Latoya as angels.

Herma: Son you have the broadest imagination that's all your always having dreams!

Gavin: Mom honestly it was so real it's like it's showing me what the future holds.

Herma: If it's to happen it will and if it's not meant to be then it won't!

Scene 43.

Herma, Gavin, Wesley, Debbie and Sadie all fly off to Jamaica. At Kingston airport.

Gavin: Wow Mom! It's hot over here!

Wesley: I can't wait to go to the beach!

Debbie: School finishes at 2 o clock man this is the life!

Sadie: This is great! Where are we going now?

Herma: We will take this taxi that's your cousins Heather's car and he will take us to a place called Watermount where we will stay with nanny and grandad for a while.

Scene 44.

Herma and the children arrive at their destination.

Narrator, (God's voice.)

Five years go by Gavin is now aboy of 17 he's been back to England once and returned back to Jamaica but I feel I should speak to him and guide him on his road to protect his destiny.

Special effects.

Gavin is awoken by a strangling feeling in his sleep.

Narrator, (God's voice.)

Wake up Gavin, don't be frightened it's me the Lord God Jehovah that is calling on you!

Gavin: Is that really you? Lord God Jehovah?

Yes it is me young Gavin, God of heaven and Earth and all creations as we know it I'm about to trace your ancestory so don't be frightened for I am here with you now!

Gavin: Mom, God spoke to me last night.

Herma: Go away Gavin!

Gavin: Honestly mom God spoke to me he said my bloodline is from Adam and Eve and went straight through all the names of the prophets until he came right to me.

It is me Gavin.

Gavin looks around but doesn't see anyone.

Gavin: Did you hear that?

Herma: No not a thing, I'm off to work see you later.

Gavin goes up to the pig pen to feed 13 pigs. They are all talking to each other.

1st pig: Do you think he's going to feed us?

2nd pig: Maybe he's tricking us maybe I'll bite him and teach him a lesson!

3rd pig: Gavin do you want to take us to slaughter? NO CHANCE!

4th pig: Sausages and bacon you should be so lucky!

Gavin: Stop it now! Just fucking stop!

Gavin puts his hands over his ears,

5th pig: When you gonna feed us? Feed us?

Gavin: I can't believe this I'm hearing what the pigs are saying! It's a miracle I must be Jesus or something!

6th pig: Do you really believe we have demons inside us?

Gavin: No, I believe pork is the sacred meat.

7th pig: Just feed us now and water us we are all very hungry!

Scene 45.

Narrator, (God's voice.)

Gavin has been awake now for a period of three weeks having the occasional nap here and there. I told him not to be frightened but I suppose that was too much to ask.

Herma: I'm taking Gavin to a psychiatric hospital Wesley he isn't well at all!

Wesley: Not well! He is totally out of his head mom first he said God spoke to him then he's preaching to people in the community telling then how to run their lives.

Herma: Your right! We will get him help fast I'll phone William he will take us in the van.

Scene 46.

Narrator, (God's voice.)

Gavin is in Spanish town trying to direct the traffic up and down the road, preaching the words of God. Jamaican police run out to him and hit him in the head with a baseball bat and beat him. Gavin is then rushed to a psychiatric hospital in an ambulance with his mother Herma by his side. Gavin is unconsious.

Scene 47.

Bellevue hospital, Kingston, Jamaica. Gavin wakes up.

Gavin: Where am I mom?

Herma: It's alright son, looks like that hit on the head knocked some sense into you.

Gavin: Mom where are you going? Mom? Please don't leave me here come back! COME BACK!

www.ingramcontent.com/pod-product-compliance
Lightning Source LLC
Chambersburg PA
CBHW060225290526
45789CB00003B/1414